westermann

W0395370

NOTTING HILL GATE

Wortschatztrainer 6

Erarbeitet von:
Christina Wolkenhauer (Rosenow)

Notting Hill Gate 6
Wortschatztrainer

Materialien zu Notting Hill Gate 6

Für Lehrkräfte:

- Textbook für Lehrkräfte 6 (ISBN 978-3-14-128285-6)
- Materialien für Lehrkräfte 6 (ISBN 978-3-14-128295-5)
- Lernerfolgskontrollen 6 (ISBN 978-3-14-128321-1)
- CD für Lehrkräfte 6 (ISBN 978-3-14-128305-1)
- DVD für Lehrkräfte 6 (ISBN 978-3-14-128315-0)
- Online-Diagnose zu Notting Hill Gate 6
  www.onlinediagnose.de

Für Schülerinnen und Schüler:

- Textbook 6 (ISBN 978-3-14-128201-6)
- Workbook 6 (inkl. Audios) (ISBN 978-3-14-128211-5)
- Interaktive Übungen 6 (WEB-14-128221)
- Arbeitsbuch Inklusion 6 (inkl. Audios)
  (ISBN 978-3-14-128231-3)
- Klassenarbeitstrainer 6 (ISBN 978-3-14-128247-4)
- Grammatiktrainer 6 (ISBN 978-3-14-128387-7)

Das digitale Schulbuch und digitale Unterrichtsmaterialien für Schülerinnen und Schüler und für Lehrkräfte finden Sie in der BiBox – dem digitalen Unterrichtssystem passend zum Lehrwerk.
Mehr Informationen über aktuelle Lizenzen finden Sie auf www.bibox.schule.

www.westermann.de/nhg

DIGITAL+

Alle digitalen Ergänzungen erkennen Sie an an dem Symbol DIGITAL+.
Dazu zählen die Videoclips.
Gehen Sie auf www.westermann.de/webcode
und geben Sie den Webcode WES-128241-001 ein. Sie können auch den QR-Code scannen.

Druck A[1] / Jahr 2023
Alle Drucke der Serie A sind im Unterricht parallel verwendbar.

Redaktion: Doris Bos
Illustrationen: Ulf Marckwort, Kassel
Umschlaggestaltung: LIO Design GmbH, Braunschweig
Layout: LIO Design GmbH, Braunschweig
Druck und Bindung: Westermann Druck GmbH, Braunschweig

ISBN 978-3-14-128241-2

Welcome to Notting Hill Gate

Einleitung .... page 4

Unit 1 Holidays

Part A Holiday fun .... page 6
Part B Sightseeing in London .... page 12

Unit 2 Celebrations

Part A Festivals and traditions .... page 18
Part B Let's celebrate! .... page 23

Unit 3 Living together

Part A Getting along .... page 26
Part B Take care! .... page 31

Unit 4 The future

Part A My dreams .... page 36
Part B Stories .... page 41

Unit 5 Out and about

Part A A trip to the museum .... page 46
Part B A play .... page 50

Wordbanks

Holidays .... page 54
Getting around .... page 56
Celebrations .... page 57
Rules .... page 58
Talking about conflicts .... page 59
Wildlife .... page 60
Jobs / Talking about the future .... page 61
Describing people .... page 62
Good style .... page 63

Lerntipps .... page 64

Liebe/r ______________________________,
(Trage hier deinen Namen ein.)

hier hältst du deinen neuen *Notting Hill Gate* Wortschatztrainer in der Hand. Du kannst damit selbstständig zu Hause arbeiten.

Der *Notting Hill Gate* Wortschatztrainer soll dir helfen, wichtige Vokabeln aus diesem Schuljahr noch einmal zu üben. Zu den Lernwörtern deines Schulbuchs findest du hier viele verschiedene Aufgaben und spannende Rätsel. Hinten im Heft findest du noch Übungen zu Vokabeln aus den *Wordbanks*, die du dort wiederholen und festigen kannst. Für viele dieser Seiten gibt es auch Videoclips, die du online abrufen kannst.

Lerntipps und Hinweise unterstützen dich beim Wortschatztraining.
Viele dieser Tipps findest du noch einmal gesammelt auf der letzten Seite dieses Hefts.
Probiere alle Tipps mehrmals aus. Nur so kannst du herausfinden, wie du persönlich am besten lernst und was dir am meisten Spaß macht.

> In diesen Kästen findest du nützliche **Lerntipps** und **Hinweise**, die dich beim Wortschatztraining unterstützen. !

Beim Vokabellernen solltest du die Zeit im Blick behalten. Es ist besser, täglich zehn Minuten zu üben als beispielsweise alle zwei Wochen zwei Stunden.

Bearbeite die Übungen im *Notting Hill Gate* Wortschatztrainer nach den zugehörigen Aufgaben aus dem Unterricht. So kannst du den Wortschatz optimal wiederholen und üben.

Neben der Aufgabennummer findest du eine Angabe zur entsprechenden Seite und Aufgabe im Textbook.

2 textbook p. 12,1

Die Vokabeln, die du in dieser Aufgabe übst, kommen direkt an dieser Stelle in deinem Schulbuch vor oder sind schon davor geübt worden und werden jetzt wiederholt.

Wenn du einmal nicht sicher bist, kannst du dir im Vokabelanhang deines Schulbuchs Hilfe holen.

Mit den Lösungen im digitalen Heft kannst du deine Antworten überprüfen.

> Alle digitalen Ergänzungen zum Buch erkennst du an dem Symbol DIGITAL+. Dazu zählen das Lösungsheft zu diesem Wortschatztrainer und viele *Wordbank*-Videoclips.
> Gehe auf www.westermann.de/webcode und gib den Webcode WES-128241-001 ein. Du kannst auch den QR-Code scannen.

Wie arbeitest du mit dem *Notting Hill Gate* Wortschatztrainer?

Schritt 1: Vorbereitung

- Wähle die Aufgaben aus, die den Wortschatz trainieren, den du gerade neu gelernt hast, und notiere dir, wann du mit dem Üben beginnst.

Schritt 2: Durchführung

- Löse die Aufgaben.
- Sieh an der entsprechenden Stelle im Kapitel oder in deinem Schulbuch in den Wortlisten ab Seite 197 nach, falls dir Vokabeln nicht einfallen.

Schritt 3: Kontrolle

- Kontrolliere nun jede Aufgabe mithilfe des Lösungshefts. Dieser Schritt ist ganz wichtig!
- Verbessere die Wörter, die du nicht richtig geschrieben hast. Trage die Wörter nach, die noch fehlen.
  Benutze hierfür eine andere Stiftfarbe, damit du auf den ersten Blick siehst, was dir noch schwergefallen ist.
- Wörter, die du nicht richtig geschrieben oder nicht gewusst hast, solltest du noch mal auf einen Zettel oder in dein Vokabelheft schreiben, damit du sie dir besser einprägen kannst.

Zum Schluss:

- Wenn du fertig bist, notiere wieder die Uhrzeit. So hast du im Blick, wie lange du geübt hast. Denke daran: Zehn Minuten jeden Tag sind besser als zwei Stunden alle zwei Wochen!

Viel Spaß und Erfolg mit dem
Notting Hill Gate **Wortschatztrainer!**

New words and phrases

1 textbook p. 8, 1

Fill in the missing words. Trage die fehlenden Wörter ein.

1 Nach der Schule will ich **ins Ausland gehen**. After school I want to ______.

2 Sie fliegt mit dem **Flugzeug** in den Urlaub.

She goes on holiday by ______.

3 Wir hatten ein tolles Hotel am **Meer** mit einer wundervollen **Aussicht**. Ich fand es **einfach** toll!

We had a great hotel at the ______ with a wonderful ______.

I ______ loved it!

4 Meine Schwester **verbringt** viel Zeit vor dem Spiegel und sie **gibt** viel Geld für Makeup **aus**.

My sister ______ a lot of time in front of the mirror and she

______ a lot of money on make-up.

5 Hallo **Leute**! Ich mag **Brettspiele** und ich **besuche** gern meine **Verwandten** in den **USA**. Ich **lerne** viel über die **Vereinigten Staaten von Amerika**.

Hi ______! I like ______ and I like ______ my

______ in the ______.

I ______ a lot about the ______.

Lerne Verben **zusammen mit möglichen Verbindungen**! Zum einen weißt du dann gleich, wie sie verwendet werden, zum anderen kannst du sie dir leichter merken, weil sie vielleicht auch Bilder im Kopf hervorrufen. Woran denkst du z. B. bei „spend money"?

Word snakes

2 textbook p. 9, 2

Find the phrases in the word snake and write them down.
Finde die Ausdrücke in der Wortschlange und schreibe sie auf.

goswimming|makefriendsgoridinglikedoingdosportsgocyclingspendmoney

______

______

Words and pictures

3 textbook p. 9, 2

Write the right words under the pictures. Schreibe die richtigen Wörter unter die Bilder.

Scrambled words

4 textbook p. 9, 2

Unscramble the words and complete the sentences with them.
Ordne die Wörter und vervollständige die Sätze mit ihnen.

1 Our dog is really ______ (y – l – a – z). He sleeps all day.

2 At ______ (i – f – s – r – t) he had breakfast, then he got dressed.

3 "I'm not going ______ (h – n – y – w – a – e – e – r)!" said my little sister.

4 There were no more seats on the bus, so I had to ______ (d – a – s – t – n).

5 The bus always ______ (a – e – s – l – v – e) from the school.

6 Will Dad ______ (c – a – n – e – h – g) his mind and let me go to the party?

7 ______ (Y – y – e – e – t – s – r – d – a) we visited the zoo and today we go swimming.

8 I'm new here, I'm here for the first ______ (e – m – i – t).

Matching pairs

5 textbook p. 9, 2

Find the matching phrases and write them down. Finde die passenden Ausdrücke und schreibe sie auf.

go · do · go · make · go · be · go · be

sports · cycling · friends · riding · good at · afraid of · abroad · swimming

Vowels

6a textbook p. 12, 6

Add the vowels *a* and *e* to the following words. Füge die Vokale *a* und *e* den folgenden Wörtern hinzu.

f r _ s h

c _ s t l _

h _ r d

c o m p _ r _

s p _ c _

_ g o

_ m _ z i n g

n _ g _ t i v _

6b

Complete the sentences with the words from a). Vervollständige die Sätze mit den Wörtern aus a).

1 Another word for 'difficult' is ____________, another word for 'great' is ____________ .

2 When I look at your text and you look at my text, we ____________ our texts.

3 A ____________ is an old building with lots of rooms and lots of ____________ .

4 A ____________ banana is green or yellow, not brown.

5 The opposite of 'positive' is ____________ .

6 'Yesterday' is one day ____________ .

Double letters

7 textbook p. 12, 6

Add the double letters *ll*, *ff*, ee and *oo* to the following words.
Füge die Doppelbuchstaben *ll*, *ff*, ee und *oo* den folgenden Wörtern hinzu.

a c t u a _ _ y

s t u _ _

b e g _ _ d a t s o m e t h i n g

s _ _ y o u s _ _ n

a _ _ t h e t i m e

d i _ _ i c u l t

Crossword

8 textbook p. 14, 9

Solve the crossword. Löse das Kreuzworträtsel.

1 If you like your food you think it is ...
2 Can you ... a car?
3 not negative
4 When you have to write three sentences or more, you have to write ... three sentences.
5 They ... from London to Manchester.
6 When something is in the way you have to ... it
7 another word for 'go by bike'
8 The parents of my parents are my ...
9 There are lots of planes at an ...
10 1 ... is about 1.6 kilometres.
11 too
12 some = a ... of
13 not a lot = a ...
14 When you work from 4 to 5, you work ... an hour.
15 to put information on the Internet
16 the opposite of 'up'
17 When you sit on a beach you sit ... the seaside.

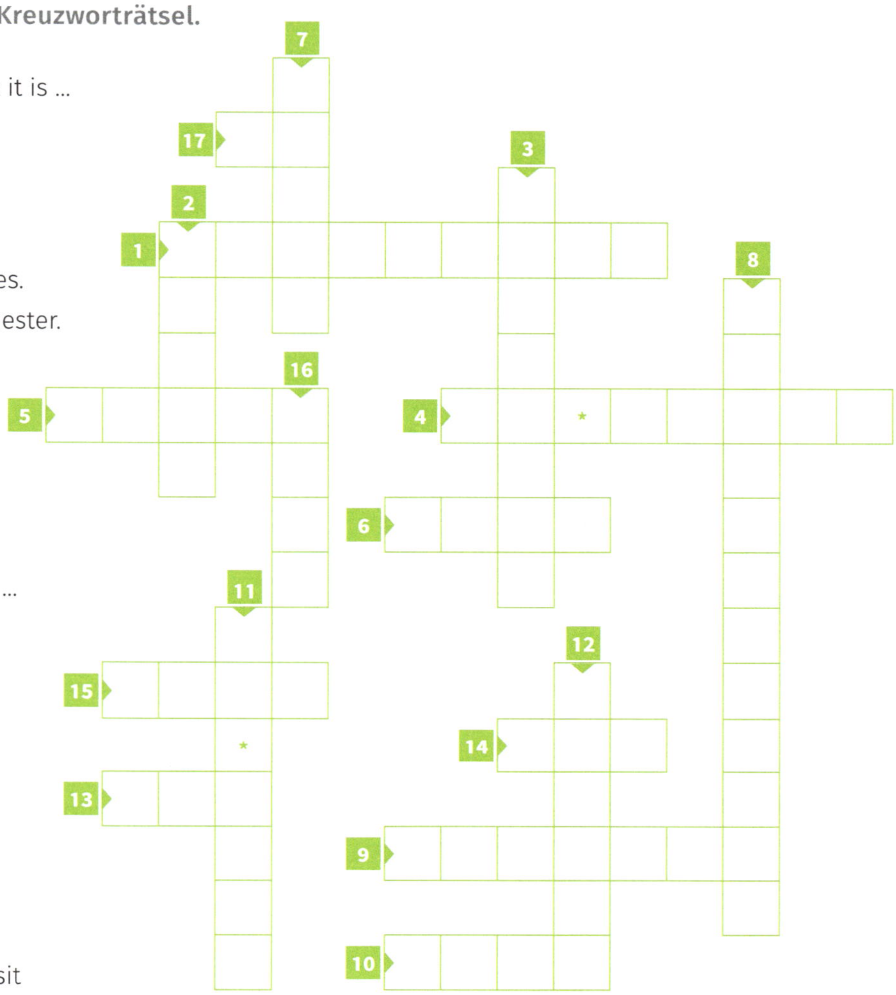

Words and pictures

9 textbook p. 14, 9

Write the right nouns under the pictures. Schreibe die richtigen Hauptwörter unter die Bilder.

Words

10 textbook p.14,9

What are the words in the box in English? Find them in the grid. → ↓ What do they have in common?
Wie heißen die Wörter im Kasten auf Englisch? Finde sie im Gitter. → ↓ Was haben sie gemeinsam?

S	C	E	N	Z	E	T	S	U	N	G	A
Y	O	U	R	S	Y	H	H	A	D	E	R
A	U	G	A	I	U	R	T	O	I	F	O
S	L	R	E	A	B	O	U	T	U	R	U
U	D	H	G	D	O	U	M	Y	X	O	N
E	E	O	N	S	P	G	K	E	T	E	D
T	G	I	A	M	K	H	Z	D	R	M	N
T	H	O	U	S	A	N	D	F	I	A	U

deine, eure, ihre
ungefähr
konnte, konntest, konnten
um, herum, umher
tausend
durch

Odd one out

11 textbook p,15,11

Find the odd one out.
Finde das Wort, das nicht zu den anderen passt.

1 around – along – taste – about
2 horrible – great – amazing – fine
3 have fun – diary entry – go hiking – meet friends
4 hill – bike – camp – might
6 down – around – by – meet
8 post – taste – along – meet

Bei diesen Aufgaben muss man manchmal nach inhaltlichen Unterschieden gucken, manchmal aber auch nach sprachlichen. Gucke dir genau an, ob die Wörter Verben, Hauptwörter, Präpositionen oder Adjektive sind! Was bedeuten sie?

5 Rome – London – Bristol – Roman
7 anyway – might – would – could
9 airport – have fun – mile – bike

Consonants

12 textbook p.16,12

Add the consonants *d*, *g*, *n*, *r* or *t* to the following words.
Füge die Konsonanten *d*, *g*, *n*, *r* oder *t* zu den folgenden Wörtern hinzu.

a f _ e _ w a _ _ s
u _ f o _ u _ a _ e l y
_ u _ i _ _
s _ _ a _ _ e

New words and phrases

13 textbook p. 17, 14

Fill in the missing words. Trage die fehlenden Wörter ein.

1 Im Zoo sind **echte** Tiere. In the zoo there are __________ animals.

2 Sarah mag Früchte, aber **besonders** Äpfel. Sarah likes fruit, but __________ apples.

3 Unser Hund schläft immer im Park. Das ist **lustig**.

Our dog always sleeps in the park. That's __________.

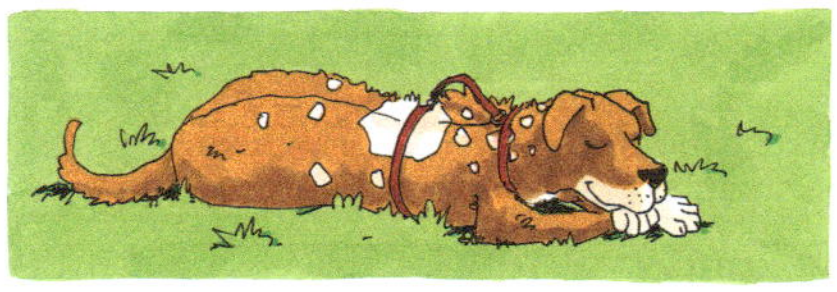

4 Der Mann im Obstladen ist immer sehr **höflich**.

The man in the fruit shop is always very __________.

5 Wenn man etwas liebt, mag man es **sehr**. If you love something, you like it __________.

6 **'Sonderbar'** und **'bewegt'** sind **Adjektive**, **'unglücklicherweise'** ist ein Adverb.

__________ and __________ are __________,

__________ is an adverb.

7 Deine **Meinung** ist das, was du denkst. Your __________ is what you think.

Nouns, verbs and adjectives

Wörterbücher gibt es auch **online** oder als **App**. Du kannst dir oft nicht nur Übersetzungen anzeigen lassen, sondern dir sogar anhören, wie ein Wort ausgesprochen wird. Außerdem findest du hinter dem Wort die phonetische Lautschrift, die dir zeigt, wie das Wort ausgesprochen wird.

14 textbook p. 17, 14

Match the words from the box to their phonetic symbols and write them down. What are they in German?
Ordne die Wörter aus dem Kasten ihrer phonetischen Lautschrift zu und schreibe sie auf. Was bedeuten sie auf Deutsch?

~~organize~~ · respect · recommend · comment on · tip · careful · polite · culture · publish · title

1	/ˈɔːɡənaɪz/	organize – organisieren	6	/ˈpʌblɪʃ/	
2	/tɪp/		7	/ˈtaɪtl/	
3	/ˈkʌltʃə/		8	/pəˈlaɪt/	
4	/rɪˈspekt/		9	/ˈkeəfl/	
5	/ˌrekəˈmend/		10	/ˈkɒment‿ɒn/	

Crossword puzzle

1 textbook p. 19, 1

Solve the crossword. Löse das Kreuzworträtsel.

1 Germany, France and Poland are in …
2 A bike has two of them, a car has four.
3 a very big and expensive house
4 The place where you live is your …
5 part of a church tower that can make sounds
6 the planet we live on
7 where people come together to decide about a country
8 very, very big
9 running water in a town or land
10 large
11 When an entry doesn't cost anything, it is …
12 You use this word when you compare something. or someone.

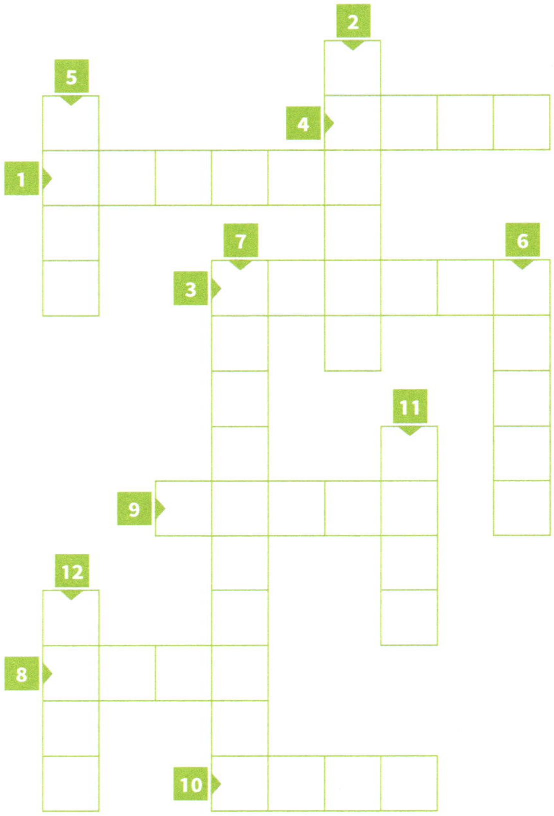

Vowels

2a textbook p. 19, 1

Add the vowels *ee*, *ea* and *ou* to the following words.
Füge die Vokale *ee*, *ea* und *ou* den folgenden Wörtern hinzu.

w h _ _ l
s _ _ n d
q u _ _ n
a l t h _ _ g h
f r _ _
_ _ r t h
h _ _ r t

2b

Choose some of the words and write sentences. Wähle einige der Wörter aus und schreibe Sätze.

New words and phrases

3 textbook p. 19, 1

Fill in the missing words. Trage die fehlenden Wörter ein.

1 Eine Giraffe ist **so** groß **wie** ein Baum. A giraffe is ____________ big ____________ a tree.

2 Gestern **entdeckte** ich einen Hund auf einem **Turm**.

Yesterday I ____________ a dog on a ____________.

3 Bist du **jemals** in London gewesen? Have you ____________ been to London?

4 Gespenster **existieren** nicht. Ghosts don't ____________.

5 Der Park ist für **die Öffentlichkeit**. The park is for ____________.

6 Ein Hund ist kleiner **als** ein Pferd. A dog is smaller ____________ a horse.

7 Das Wort **'königlich'** hat mit einem **König** oder einer **Königin** zu tun. The word ____________

has to do with a ____________ or a ____________.

8 **Britische** Menschen kommen aus dem **Vereinigten Königreich**. Sie müssen reisen, um nach Frankreich zu **kommen**. ____________ people come from the ____________.

They have to travel to ____________ to France.

Words

4 textbook p. 19, 1

What are the nouns in the box in English? Find them in the grid. → ↓ ←

Wie heißen die Hauptwörter im Kasten auf Englisch? Finde sie im Gitter. → ↓ ←

A	E	B	T	T	L	U	D	A	M	N	I
A	T	T	R	A	C	T	I	O	N	E	R
T	S	R	U	O	S	S	S	I	M	O	S
E	E	X	H	I	B	I	T	I	O	N	T
N	N	B	I	M	E	E	O	R	D	D	A
T	G	N	I	D	L	I	U	B	E	B	I
R	E	R	O	T	B	O	N	T	L	S	R
Y	S	E	I	C	E	P	S	P	O	T	A

Modell
oberes Ende, Spitze
Eintritt
Stufe
Gebäude
Attraktion
Ausstellung
Art, Spezies
Erwachsene/r

Scrambled words

5 textbook p. 20

Unscramble the words and complete the sentences and questions with them.
Ordne die Wörter und vervollständige die Sätze und Fragen mit ihnen.

1 The ______________ (w – r – o – t – s) team in a match doesn't play as well as the ______________ (s – t – e – b) team.

2 A ______________ (g – r – b – e – d – i) is a road over a river.

3 Things are very different ______________ (o – y – d – t – a) from what they were in the past.

4 A mobile in a baby's room has many ______________ (v – m – n – g – o – i) parts. Mobiles are very ______________ (p – r – p – u – o – a – l).

5 Do you watch TV every night ______________ (l – t – n – i – u) you must go to bed?

6 Does this shirt go ______________ (t – w – h – i) my green trousers?

Pairs

6 textbook p. 20, 2

Find the pairs in the two boxes. Write them down. **Finde die Paare in den zwei Kästen. Schreibe sie auf.**

beautiful · old · king · under · small · child · left · better

worse · large · onto · queen · right ugly · young · adult

Word snake

7 textbook p. 22, 6

Find the phrases in the word snake and write them down.
Finde die Ausdrücke in der Wortschlange und schreibe sie auf.

taketime|followdirectionswalkpastchangelinesturnleftcrosstheroadgostraighton

take time,

Classroom phrases

8 textbook p. 22, 6

Match the sentences. Ordne die Sätze zu.

1 Pay attention to the spelling.	A Beschreibe einem Partner / einer Partnerin den Weg und folge seinen / ihren Wegbeschreibungen.
2 Write down three comparisons.	B Benutze Adjektive.
3 Give directions to a partner and follow their directions.	C Achte auf die Rechtschreibung.
4 Use adjectives.	D Schreibe drei Vergleiche auf.

Words and pictures

9 textbook p. 22, 6

Write the right words under the pictures. Schreibe die richtigen Wörter unter die Bilder.

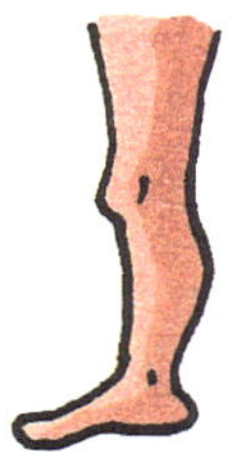

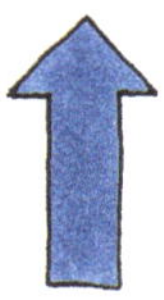

Directions

10 textbook p. 22, 6

Match the sentences.
Ordne die Sätze einander zu.

1 Follow the directions.	A Biege rechts ab.
2 Turn left onto Baker Street.	B Überquere den Fluss.
3 Turn right.	C Folge den Wegbeschreibungen.
4 Cross the river.	D Beschreibe den Weg.
5 Give directions.	E Aber du musst umsteigen, wenn du die U-Bahn nimmst.
6 Walk past the cinema.	F Dann gehe in Richtung Park.
7 Then walk towards the park.	G Gehe am Kino vorbei.
8 But you have to change lines when you take the tube.	H Biege links ab in die Baker Street.

1	2	3	4	5	6	7	8
C							

Consonants

11 textbook p. 26, 12

Add the consonants *c* or *s* to the following words.
Füge die Konsonanten *c* oder *s* den folgenden Wörtern hinzu.

1 e x p e n _ i v e

2 e n t r a n _ e

3 m u _ i _ i a n

4 l e _ _

5 v i _ i t o r

6 p o _ _ i b i l i t y

7 p r e _ e n t

8 _ o r n e r

9 g l a _ _

Schwierige Wörter
Wenn du merkst, dass du bei der Schreibweise einiger englischer Wörter Schwierigkeiten hast, kannst du sie auf ein Blatt Papier schreiben und die Stelle markieren, die dir Probleme macht. Hänge das Blatt in deinem Zimmer auf und gucke dir die Wörter immer wieder an. Du wirst merken, dass du sie bald richtig schreiben kannst.

Crossword

12 textbook p. 26, 13

Solve the crossword. Löse das Kreuzworträtsel.

1 the opposite of more

2 If you're afraid of ..., you don't go up any mountains.

3 The London Tube is an ...

4 A band plays songs for ...

5 In Wembley Stadium they play football and there is sometimes also a ...

6 two or more things together = a ... of things

7 twenty plus eighty

8 When you turn left or right, you go ... a corner.

9 noun for when a shop or museum is open: opening ...

10 From the top of a tower you can see the people ...

11 another word for tourist

12 You can put ... in a vase.

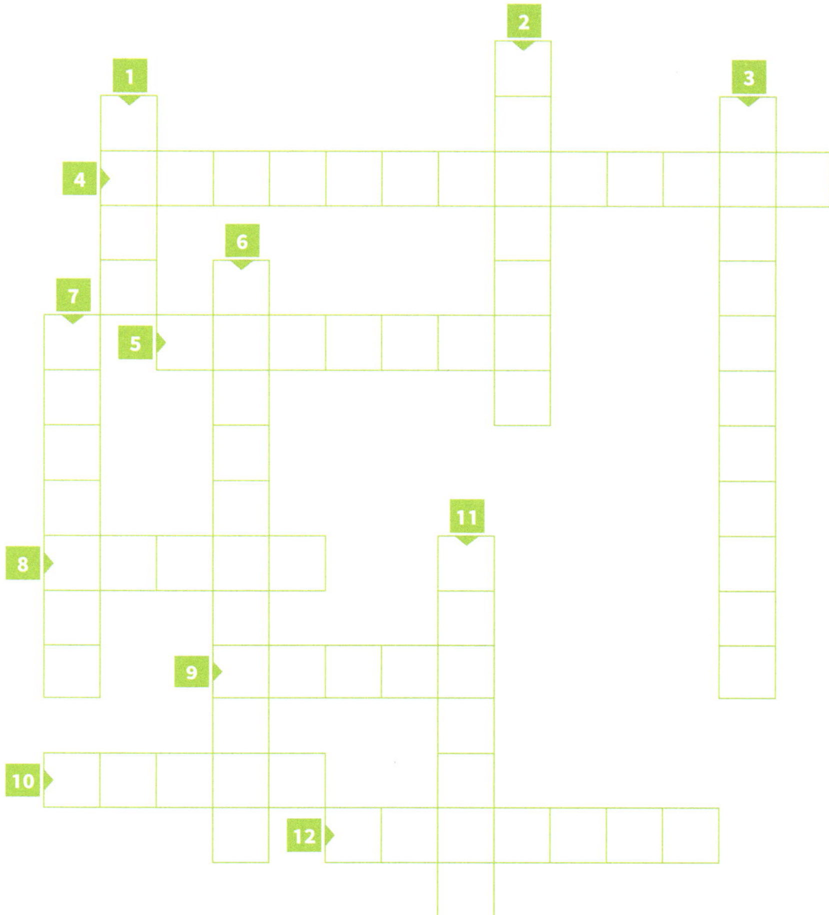

Odd one out

13 textbook p. 27, 14

Find the odd one out. Write it down and add the German meaning. Finde das Wort, dass nicht zu den anderen passt. Schreibe es auf und füge die deutsche Bedeutung hinzu.

1 whole – concert – theme – height ______

2 theme – words – sentences – letters ______

3 entry – visitor – exhibition – for free ______

4 below – less – day out – round ______

5 draft – to see – to write – to read ______

6 concert – visitor – combination – enter ______

Missing vowels

1a textbook p. 33, 1

Add the missing vowels *a, e, i, o* or *u*. Füge die fehlenden Vokale *a, e, i, o* oder *u* hinzu.

1 c _ l _ b r _ t _ _ n

2 f _ s t _ v _ l

3 s p r _ n g

4 d _ r k n _ s s

5 b _ g _ n n _ n g

6 h _ l _ d _ y

7 v _ c t _ r y

8 d _ c _ r _ t _ _ n

1b

Complete the sentences with some of the words from a).
Vervollständige die Sätze mit einigen der Wörter aus a).

1 ______________________ is between winter and summer.

2 People often buy ______________________ for parties.

3 The opposite of ending is ______________________ .

4 There is ______________________ when there is no light at night.

Word snake

2 textbook p. 33, 1

Find all the words that have to do with religion and write them down.
Finde alle Wörter, die mit Religion zu tun haben, und schreibe sie auf.

mHaChristianKuegrMuslimporprayergandJewishHelloHinduismchozdreligious

____

____

Words and pictures

3 textbook p. 33, 1

Write the words under the pictures. Schreibe die Wörter unter die Bilder.

Matching pairs

4 textbook p. 33, 1

Find the matching pairs from the two boxes and write them down.
Finde die Wörter aus den zwei Kästen, die zusammengehören, und schreibe sie auf.

~~have~~ · stand · believe · take · depend

for · place · ~~in common~~ · in · on

have in common,

Verbs

5a textbook p. 33, 1

Find six verbs in the grid. → ↓ Finde sechs Verben im Gitter.

W	C	E	L	E	B	R	A	T	E	E	D
F	I	T	E	D	R	S	I	E	D	O	M
H	E	K	L	O	I	P	A	R	L	P	O
I	R	T	A	K	E	*	P	L	A	C	E
D	A	L	P	S	D	S	K	P	S	K	N
E	S	L	I	G	H	T	L	D	T	L	D

Du kannst zum Lernen auch **Wortnetze** zu bestimmten Themen anlegen. Nimm ein Blatt Papier und schreibe das Thema, beispielsweise „Festivals“, in die Mitte. Welche Wörter passen dazu? Notiere sie und versuche, sie sinnvoll zu verbinden.

5b

Choose three of the verbs and write sentences. Wähle drei der Verben aus und schreibe Sätze.

New words and phrases

6 textbook p. 34, 2

Fill in the missing words. Trage die fehlenden Wörter ein.

1 **Chinesen** feiern **auf der ganzen Welt** das **traditionelle** Neujahr.

______ celebrate the ______ New Year ______.

2 Auf der **folgenden** Seite findest du mehr Informationen.

On the ______ page you will find more information.

3 Der Laden hat die ganze **Nacht** geöffnet.

The shop is open all ______.

4 Ich fragte ihn gestern, aber er sagte **nichts**.

I asked him yesterday, but he did ______ say ______.

5 Wenn du und deine Freundin die gleiche Kleidung mögt, **habt** ihr etwas **gemeinsam**.

If you and your friend like the same clothes, you ______ something ______.

Crossword puzzle

7 textbook p. 35, 4

Solve the crossword. Löse das Kreuzworträtsel.

1 People in Germany celebrate ... on the 24th of December.

2 On Sundays many Christians go to ...

3 You look up words in a ...

4 a small green or blue fruit

5 In Germany, a pig is a symbol for good ...

6 another word for tell

7 I want to ... the colour of my hair. It's brown now, I want to have red hair.

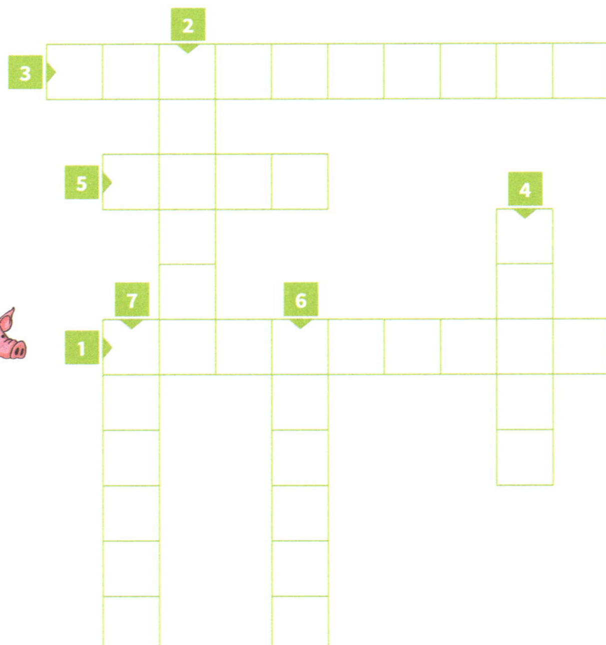

Difficult words

8a textbook p. 36, 6

Match the words from the box to their phonetic symbols.
Ordne die Wörter aus dem Kasten ihrer phonetischen Lautschrift zu.

mix · Britain · Ireland · rule · northern · ghost · offer

1 /ˈaɪələnd/ ____________

2 /mɪks/ ____________

3 /ˈnɔːðən/ ____________

4 /ɡəʊst/ ____________

5 /ˈɒfə/ ____________

6 /ruːl/ ____________

7 /ˈbrɪtn/ ____________

8b

Complete the sentences with some of the words from the box.
Vervollständige die Sätze mit einigen der Wörter aus dem Kasten.

1 People celebrate St. Patrick's Day especially in ____________ .

2 England, Scotland and Wales are parts of ____________ .

3 Some people think that there is a ____________ in every old castle.

4 You can ____________ water and apple juice and get a nice drink.

5 You usually ____________ a guest something to drink.

Consonants

9a textbook p. 38, 7

Add the consonants *c*, *p*, *s* or *y*. Füge die Konsonanten *c*, *p*, *s* oder *y* hinzu.

1 _ w e e t

2 _ r o b a b l _

3 _ _ a r _

4 _ e n t u r _

5 _ o m m e r _ i a l

6 _ t u _ i d

7 _ u r _ r i _ i n g

8 _ u m _ k i n

9b

Sort the words alphabetically. Sortiere die Wörter alphabetisch.

____

____

Scrambled words

10 textbook p. 38, 7

Unscramble the words and complete the sentences with them.
Ordne die Wörter und vervollständige die Sätze mit ihnen.

1 I think Halloween today is very ______ (o – c – m – e – m – r – l – c – a – i).

2 I don't like dressing up. I think it's ______ (d – s – t – i – u – p).

3 Costume ______ (n – m – e – a – s) 'Kostüm' in German.

4 My favourite ______ (r – e – h – c – a – a – t – r – c) in my new book is Mia.

5 You can cook a nice dessert ______ (u – o – t) of apples.

6 On Halloween many people carve lanterns out of ______ (s – p – k – p – i – u – m – n).

7 I have all ______ (n – s – k – d – i) of hobbies: volleyball, swimming and reading.

Opposites

11 textbook p. 41, 12

Find the opposite pairs in the two boxes and write them down.
Finde die Gegensatzpaare in den zwei Kästen und schreibe sie auf.

> **Gegensätze**
> Neue Vokabeln kannst du dir auch gut merken, wenn du sie dir mit ihren Gegensätzen zusammenstellst und als Gegensatzpaar lernst.

con · to empty · outside · together · to put down

inside · to fill · pro · apart · to put up

______

______

______

Odd one out

12 textbook p. 41, 12

Find the odd one out. Finde das Wort, das nicht zu den anderen passt.

1 pumpkin – Halloween – ghost – piece
2 cut – decoration – balloon – candle
3 surprising – commercial – make sure – stupid
4 jack-o'-lantern – apple bobbing – pumpkins – category
5 Ireland – country – Britain – USA
6 history – PE – background – geography

Vowels

1 textbook p. 44, 5

Add the vowels *a*, *e*, *i*, *o* or *u* to the following words. Find the German meaning and draw lines.
Füge die Buchstaben *a*, *e*, *i*, *o* oder *u* den folgenden Wörtern hinzu. Finde die deutsche Bedeutung und verbinde die Wörter.

r _ l _	Betonung
j _ _ n _ n	draußen
m _ y	ziemlich
s t r _ s s	so
q _ _ t _	können, dürfen
t h _ t	Rolle
_ _ t	sich beteiligen an

New words and phrases

2 textbook p. 45, 6

Fill in the missing words. Trage die fehlenden Wörter ein.

1 **Sieh dir** das schöne Foto **an**. ______________________ the beautiful photo.

2 Es ist der 22. Dezember. Es ist **fast** Weihnachten.

It's the 22nd of December. It's ______________ Christmas.

3 Was gibt es Weihnachten bei euch? Wir wissen es **noch nicht**.

What do you have for Christmas? We do ______________ know ______________.

4 Heute Abend läuft ein Fußballspiel im Fernsehen. Das werde ich **definitiv** schauen.

Tonight there is a football match on TV. I'll ______________ watch it.

5 Sue und Emma **werden** morgen einen Test schreiben.

Sue and Emma ______________ do a test tomorrow.

Words and pictures

Achtung, hier werden unterschiedliche Wortarten gesucht!

3 textbook p. 45, 6

Write the right words under the pictures.

____

____

____

____

A note from Sandra

4 textbook p. 46, 7

Complete Sandra's note with the words from the box.
Vervollständige Sandras Nachricht mit den Wörtern aus dem Kasten.

Hi Mia,

It's ______________ Saturday and I wanted to tell you about our party.

We collected a lot of ______________ for the ______________.

My mum and dad are going to ______________ some delicious food.

We are going to have a ______________ with lots of jacket potatoes.

It's going to be the best Bonfire Party ever. See you on Saturday?

______________,

Sandra

wood · almost · cook · fire · Love · bowl

Odd one out

5 textbook p. 46, 7

Find the odd one out. Finde das Wort, das nicht zu den anderen passt.

1 bananas – sugar – apples – carrots
2 pencil – felt-tip – pen – sheet
3 big – tall – a little – huge
4 order – to remove – to push – to leave
5 bowl – sugar – should – order

Die Strategien, die du beim Lösen dieser Aufgaben nutzt, kannst du auch zum Vokabellernen verwenden: Erstelle in einem Ordner **Tabellen** mit **Oberbegriffen** zu bestimmten Themen. Sammle Wörter, die zum Oberbegriff passen.

Crossword

6 textbook p. 47, 8

Solve the crossword. Löse das Kreuzworträtsel.

1 A long shirt ... your arms.
2 to put away = to ...
3 the opposite of to pull: to ...
4 You can find information ... using the Internet.
5 You ... do your homework.
6 ... your mobile at home when you go swimming!
7 Don't jump into the pool for your own ...!

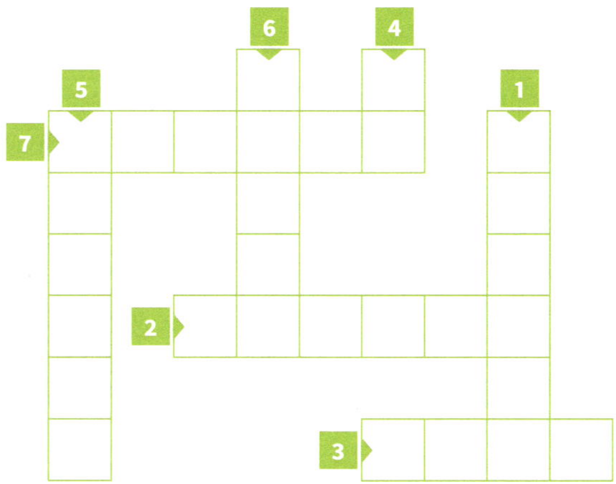

What you write and what you hear

7a textbook p. 51, 16

Match the words from the box to their phonetic symbols.
Ordne die Wörter aus dem Kasten ihrer phonetischen Lautschrift zu.

1 /ˈsʌmweə/ ____________

2 /ˈhelθi/ ____________

3 /ˈɜːliə/ ____________

4 /riˈækʃn/ ____________

5 /ˈriːzn/ ____________

6 /ˈɔːtəm/ ____________

reaction · reason · earlier · healthy · autumn · somewhere

7b

Choose four of the words and write sentences.
Wähle vier der Wörter aus und schreibe Sätze.

____

____

____

____

Words with double letters

8a textbook p. 51, 16

The double letters from the words in the box are missing. Find the right letters and write down the words. **Die Doppelbuchstaben der Wörter im Kasten fehlen. Finde die richtigen Buchstaben und schreibe die Wörter auf.**

~~stre??~~ · sh??t · discu?? · w??d · su??estion · discu??ion

stress, ____________

____

8b

Complete the sentences with some of the words from the box.
Vervollständige die Sätze mit einigen der Wörter aus dem Kasten.

1 Take out a ____________ of paper.

2 My desk is made out of ____________. It's brown.

3 Let's ____________ the problem.

4 What do we do? Do you have a ____________?

Matching pairs

1a textbook p. 57, 1

Find the words that belong together and write them down.
Finde die Wörter, die zusammengehören, und schreibe sie auf.

> ! Lerne **Verben** möglichst immer zusammen **mit** den **zugehörigen Präpositionen**. Das hilft dir beim Bilden von Sätzen.

get · take care · be allowed · shout

of · along · at · to

____

____

1b

Complete the sentences with the words from a). Vervollständige die Sätze mit den Wörtern aus a).

1 Ich hoffe, dass ich **mich** mit meinen neuen Klassenkameraden **verstehen** werde.

I hope I will ______________ with my new classmates.

2 Ich muss **mich** jeden Freitagabend um meinen kleinen Bruder **kümmern**.

I have to ______________ my little brother every Friday afternoon.

3 Ich **darf** den neuen Actionfilm nicht sehen, weil ich nicht alt genug bin.

I ________ not ______________ watch the new action film because I'm not old enough.

4 Der Fußballtrainer **schreit** die Spieler oft **an**. Das ist nicht nett.

The football coach often ______________ the players. That's not nice.

Scrambled words

2 textbook p. 57, 1

Unscramble the words and complete the sentences with them.
Ordne die Wörter und vervollständige die Sätze mit ihnen.

1 You ________ (s – t – m – u) be polite and show ______________ (r – t – e – s – c – p – e) to your parents.

2 When you ______________ (e – r – o – p – t – r) to someone, then you tell them that you are here.

3 You ______________ (t – s – t – u – m – n') bring knives or other ______________ (n – g – u – d – o – s – r – a – e) things to school.

4 He didn't ______________ (n – r – u) fast enough to catch the bus.

5 When the teacher ______________ (e – e – n – r – t – s) the classroom, everybody is quiet.

6 I got a new ______________ (p – c – a) yesterday. It's cool, isn't it?

A word snake

3a textbook p. 57, 1

The words in the snake have lost the letters "ou", "oo" or "o". Find the words, add the letters and write down the words. Die Wörter in der Schlange haben die Buchstaben "ou", "oo" oder "o" verloren. Finde die Wörter, füge die Buchstaben hinzu und schreibe die Wörter auf.

schlgrnds/dangersknncktrblebred

____

____

____

3b

Write your own word snake. Use words from Unit 3. Let your partner guess.
Schreibe deine eigene Wortschlange. Benutze die Wörter aus Kapitel 3. Lass deinen Partner / deine Partnerin raten.

The words in my snake have lost the letters: ______________

New words and phrases

4 textbook p. 59, 6

Fill in the missing words. Trage die fehlenden Wörter ein.

1 Er **bricht** immer die Regeln. Er kommt jeden Tag zu spät.

He always ______________ the rules. He is late every day.

2 Sein **Knie** schmerzt sehr stark. Er hat gestern Fußball gespielt.

His ______________ hurts really badly. He played football yesterday.

3 **Meiner Meinung nach** ist Hockey interessanter als Jogging.

______________________________, hockey is more interesting than jogging.

4 Manche Menschen wollen ihren **Stil ausdrücken**, indem sie besondere Kleidung tragen.

Some people want to ______________ their ______________ by wearing special clothes.

5 Ich habe ein neues Paar **Schuhe**. I have a new pair of ______________.

6 Meine Großmutter mag **Schmuck** sehr gern. My grandma likes ______________ very much.

7 Ich bin froh. Ich habe eine gute **Note** in einem Test bekommen.

I'm happy. I got a good ______________ in a test.

Feelings

5a textbook p. 60, 7

Find eight words for feelings in the grid. → ↓
Finde acht Wörter für Gefühle im Gitter. → ↓

Für gute Zuhörer
Du kannst dir Vokabeln auch merken, indem du sie dir immer wieder anhörst. Nimm die englischen Wörter auf, die du dir merken willst, und vergiss die deutsche Übersetzung nicht!
Höre dir die Wörter regelmäßig an und sprich sie nach.

A	N	G	R	Y	A	S	R	G	H	Z	T	V	N	M
R	Q	E	Z	U	P	L	K	D	F	G	W	Y	C	B
M	N	H	S	W	T	T	S	A	D	F	O	A	S	W
E	R	T	A	Z	U	Z	C	B	N	V	R	M	M	R
Q	W	E	D	R	T	Z	U	I	O	P	R	A	S	F
G	H	J	K	M	Y	L	X	C	V	B	I	N	M	Q
A	S	Y	X	D	R	E	F	V	G	H	E	W	R	W
I	J	N	U	H	T	I	R	E	D	R	D	D	E	X
W	A	Y	E	D	X	T	F	C	Z	G	V	Z	L	B
I	H	N	W	A	S	Y	F	B	H	J	K	M	A	R
L	A	N	N	O	Y	E	D	Y	S	D	C	E	X	T
W	S	X	C	F	R	E	D	T	G	U	J	G	E	I
I	O	P	K	J	S	A	W	S	C	A	R	E	D	F
B	O	R	E	D	Y	A	D	R	Z	B	H	H	F	W
M	J	U	C	E	W	A	Y	X	G	P	O	X	V	B

5b

Write the right words from a) under the pictures. Schreibe die richtigen Wörter aus a) unter die Bilder.

5c

Sort the adjectives alphabetically. Can you add more?
Sortiere die Adjektive alphabetisch. Kannst du noch mehr hinzufügen?

Odd one out

6a textbook p. 62, 10

Find the odd one out. Finde das Wort, das nicht zu den anderen passt.

1 angry – bored – feel – sad
2 sign – autumn – summer – winter
3 friendship – knee – head – leg
4 write – TV – watch – hear
5 side – tie – shirt – trousers

6b

Complete the sentences with the words from a). Vervollständige die Sätze mit den Wörtern von a).

1 I would like to have a new mobile. I hope my dad is on my __________ and buys one.
2 Look for the __________. It helps you to find the way to the library.
3 I don't have a __________ in my room. There is one in our living room.
4 I __________ really good today because we are going on holiday.
5 __________ is very important to me.

Words with missing letters

7a textbook p. 63, 11

Add the letters *i* or *y* to the following words.
Füge die Buchstaben *i* oder *y* den folgenden Wörtern hinzu.

1 f _ n _ s h
2 d _ a r _
3 b _
4 s t r _ c t
5 e a r l _
6 n o t a n _ m o r e
7 w h _ l e
8 m e e t _ n g

7b

Choose four of the words and write sentences. Wähle vier der Wörter aus und schreibe Sätze.

Missing vowels

8a textbook p. 65, 15

Add the missing vowels *o* and *u*. Füge die fehlenden Vokale *o* und *u* hinzu.

1 c _ n f l i c t
2 c _ m p r _ m i s e
3 w _ r k
4 d _ _ r
5 g _ _ _ t
6 s _ l u t i _ n

8b

Complete the sentences with the words from a). Vervollständige die Sätze mit den Wörtern aus a).

1 You must sometimes make a ____________ in a ____________.
2 My smartphone doesn't ____________ anymore. It fell into the lake.
3 Please, come in. The ____________ is open.

4 I want to ____________ on Saturday. There's a party at my friend's house.
5 Often there is a ____________ to a problem.

Classroom phrases

9 textbook p. 65, 15

Match the sentences. Draw lines. Ordne die Sätze einander zu. Verbinde.

Plan your role play.	Was könnte eine Lösung sein?
What could be a solution?	Kommt in Vierergruppen zusammen.
Find a compromise.	Plant euer Rollenspiel.
Get together in groups of four.	Findet Argumente für und gegen die Benutzung von Handys im Klassenraum.
Who takes part in the role play?	Findet einen Kompromiss.
Find arguments for and against using mobile phones in classroom.	Denkt über einen Konflikt in der Familie nach.
Think about a conflict in the family.	Wer nimmt am Rollenspiel teil?

Words and pictures

1 textbook p. 66, 1

Write the right words under the pictures. Schreibe die richtigen Wörter unter die Bilder.

Missing vowels

2a textbook p. 67, 1

***O* or *e*? Add the vowels *o* or *e* to the following words.**
O oder *e*? Füge die Vokale *o* oder *e* den folgenden Wörtern hinzu.

n _ t _

b _ _ k

f _ _ d

c _ n t r _

c l _ s _ d

f _ r _ s t

l _ a d

r u n n _ r

2b

***Y* or *i*? Add the letters *y* or *i* to the following words.**
Y oder *i*? Füge die Buchstaben *y* oder *i* den folgenden Wörtern hinzu.

h _ r e

c o u n t r _ s _ d e

n o t h _ n g

w _ l d l _ f e

s u d d e n l _

t a k e a w a _

n a t _ o n a l p a r k

2c

Choose two of the words from 2a and 2b and write sentences.
Wähle zwei der Wörter aus 2a und 2b aus und schreibe Sätze.

Odd one out

3 textbook p. 67, 1

Find the odd one out. Write it down and add the German meaning. Finde das Wort, das nicht zu den anderen passt. Schreibe es auf und füge die deutsche Bedeutung hinzu.

1 shopping centre – countryside – museum – station ______

2 paint – draw – cut – photograph ______

3 safe – feed – hire – explore ______

4 explore – nature – animals – forest ______

New words and phrases

4 textbook p. 67, 1

Fill in the missing words. Trage die fehlenden Wörter ein.

1 Es gibt ein paar Regeln für unseren Besuch im **Nationalpark**.

There are some rules for our visit to the ______.

2 Ihr müsst auf einem Bauernhof immer das **Tor** hinter euch schließen.

You always have to close the ______ behind you on a farm.

3 Wenn ich mein Handy zu oft benutze, wird meine Mutter es mir **wegnehmen**.

If I use my mobile phone too often, my mum will ______ it ______.

4 Da ist **nichts** zu sehen im Käfig. Die Tiere sind draußen.

There is ______ to see in the cage. The animals are outside.

5 Ich esse nichts **außer** Früchte heute. I eat nothing ______ fruit today.

Consonants

5a textbook p. 69, 6

Add the consonants *p*, *s*, *t* or *y* to the following words.
Füge die Konsonanten *p*, *s*, *t* oder *y* den folgenden Wörtern hinzu.

1 l e _ _ e r

2 _ e a r

3 _ r i _

4 j a c k e _

5 _ e r m i _ _ i o n

6 _ a y m e n _

7 r e _ u r n

8 w r i _ _ e n

5b

Match the sentences. Ordne die Sätze einander zu.

1 Dear students,	A Mit freundlichen Grüßen
2 I'm writing this letter to inform you about our class trip.	B Ich freue mich auf einen aufregenden Ausflug.
3 Take a warm jacket.	C Liebe Schülerinnen und Schüler,
4 I'm looking forward to an exciting trip.	D Ich schreibe diesen Brief, um euch über unseren Ausflug zu informieren.
5 I need the written permission and the payment from your parents.	E Nehmt eine warme Jacke mit.
6 Yours sincerely,	F Ich brauche die schriftliche Erlaubnis und die Bezahlung von euren Eltern.

Words and pictures

6 textbook p. 71, 7

Write the words under the pictures. Schreibe die Wörter unter die Bilder.

 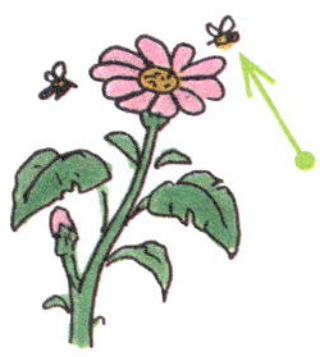    

______ ______ ______ ______ ______ ______

What's the letter?

7a textbook p. 71, 7

***D* or *t*? Add the letters *d* or *t* to the following words.**
D oder *t*? Füge die Buchstaben *d* oder *t* den folgenden Wörtern hinzu.

p r o _ e c _   _ e s _ r o y
h e _ g e h o g   _ r y
p l a n _   g r o u n _
_ a n g e r   p r o _ u c e

7b

Choose three of the words and write sentences. Wähle drei der Wörter aus und schreibe Sätze.

______

______

______

Scrambled words

8 textbook p. 71, 7

Unscramble the words and complete the sentences with them.
Ordne die Wörter und vervollständige die Sätze mit ihnen.

1 My best friend gets money when she does __________ (o – b – j – s) at home, for example when she washes the car.

2 My mobile always falls on the __________. (o – g – r – d – u – n)

3 My mum __________ (w – s – g – r – o) vegetables in the garden.

4 Our new __________ (r – j – p – e – c – o – t) at school is about pets.

5 A __________ (f – i – n – d – l – r – e – y) person is really nice.

6 There are a lot of cars and bikes on __________ (y – u – s – b) roads.

New words and phrases

Mache sie du deinen Wörtern!
Am besten kannst du dir Wörter merken, die du selbst verwendet hast. Bilde eigene Sätze mit den Wörtern, die du dir merken sollst. Sie können auch lustig sein oder sich reimen.

9 textbook p. 74, 12

Fill in the missing words. **Trage die fehlenden Wörter ein.**

1 Lies die **Anweisungen**. Dann weißt du, wie man es baut.

Read the __________. Then you know how to build it.

2 Zwei ist die **Hälfte** von vier.

Two is __________ of four.

3 Du brauchst eine **Schnur**, um die Futterstation **aufzuhängen**.

You need a __________ to __________ the bird feeder.

4 Wir **hängten** ein großes Bild vom letzten Urlaub an der **Wand** im Wohnzimmer **auf**.

We __________ a big picture from our last holiday on the __________ in the living room.

5 Die **Umwelt** ist alles, was mit Natur zu tun hat.

The __________ is anything to do with nature.

Crossword puzzle

10 textbook p. 75, 14

Solve the crossword. Löse das Kreuzworträtsel.

1 another word for nature
2 another word for task
3 I always put ... in my apple juice to make it colder.
4 the opposite of 'on'
5 Do you ... the hedgehog over there?
6 to be a part of or to make somebody a part of
7 a person who knows a lot about a special topic
8 the opposite of 'wet'

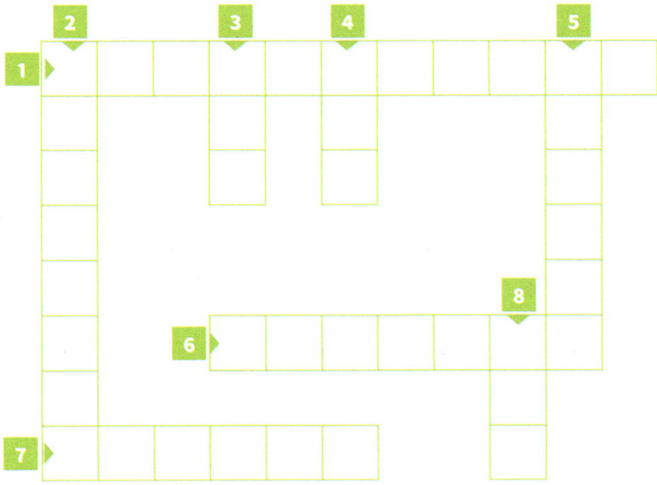

Word snakes

11a textbook p. 75, 14

The words in the word snake have lost the letters *ex*. Find them, add the letters and write them down.
Die Wörter in der Wortschlange haben die Buchstaben *ex* verloren. Finde sie, füge die Buchstaben hinzu und schreibe sie auf.

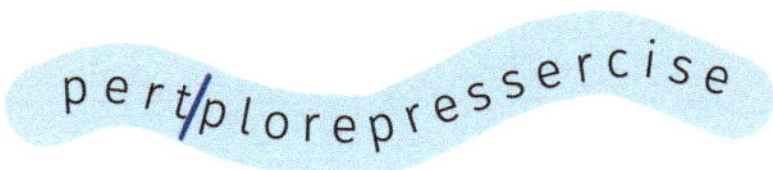

11b

The words in the word snake have lost the letter *y*. Find them, add the letter and write them down.
Die Wörter in der Wortschlange haben den Buchstaben *y* verloren. Finde sie, füge den Buchstaben hinzu und schreibe sie auf.

New words and phrases

1 textbook p. 80, 1

Fill in the missing words. Trage die fehlenden Wörter ein.

1 Letztes Jahr liegt in der Vergangenheit und das nächste Jahr liegt in der **Zukunft**.

Last year is in the past and next year is in the ______________.

2 Unser Urlaub war ein **Abenteuer**. Er war toll!

Our holiday was an ______________. It was great!

3 Nächstes Jahr **werden** wir ein Video in der Schule **drehen**. Ich freue mich darauf.

Next year we ______________ ______________ a video in school. I'm looking forward to it.

4 Ich mag unsere **öffentliche** Bibliothek sehr. Dort kann man tolle Bücher ausleihen.

I like our ______________ library very much. You can borrow wonderful books there.

5 **Entweder gibt** Sue ihre Hausaufgaben bis morgen **ab oder** der Lehrer informiert ihre Eltern.

______________ Sue ______________ ______________ her homework by tomorrow

______________ her teacher will inform her parents.

Vowels

2a textbook p. 81, 2

Add the vowels *a, e, i, o* or *u* to the following words. Add the German meaning.
Füge die Vokale *a, e, i, o* oder *u* den folgenden Wörtern hinzu. Füge die deutsche Bedeutung hinzu.

d r _ w _ n g ______________

w h _ t _ v _ r ______________

l _ _ v _ ______________

c _ n t _ c t ______________

r _ g _ l _ r ______________

c _ s t _ m _ r ______________

2b

Complete the sentences with the words from a). Vervollständige die Sätze mit den Wörtern aus a).

1 Little children often give their parents a ______________. 2 On my birthday I can do ______________ I want to do. 3 A ______________ is a person who buys something. 4 Please ______________ your email address and I will ______________ you. 5 The opposite of 'special' is ______________.

Odd one out

3 textbook p. 81, 2

Find the odd one out. Finde das Wort, das nicht zu den anderen passt.

1 fashion – hedgehog – squirrel – bird
2 car – invent – dishwasher – mobile phone
3 exercise book – engineer – pen – ruler
4 honest – bad – wrong – false
5 beautiful – great – wonderful – grow up
6 contact – drawing – singer – and so on

Consonants

4 textbook p. 83, 6

***C* or *g*? Add the consonants *c* or *g* to the following words.**
C oder *g*? Füge die Konsonanten *c* oder *g* den folgenden Wörtern zu.

1 s i n _ e r
2 e x a _ t l y
3 s t a _ e
4 p o l i _ e   o f f i _ e r
5 a _ t r e s s
6 t e _ h n o l o _ y
7 m e _ h a n i _
8 a _ t

Double consonants

5 textbook p. 83, 6

***Th*, *gh* or *ch*? Add the letters *th*, *gh* or *ch* to the following words.**
Th, *gh* oder *ch*? Füge die Buchstaben *th*, *gh* oder *ch* den folgenden Wörtern zu.

1 f i _ _ t
2 e i _ _ e r   o r
3 r a _ _ e r   _ _ a n
4 t e _ _ n o l o g y

Jobs

6 textbook p. 85, 9

Write the words under the pictures.
Schreibe die Wörter unter die Bilder.

Verknüpfungen herstellen
Bei Wörtern, die du dir überhaupt nicht merken kannst, kannst du
- ein kleines Bild dazu zeichnen,
- einen Satz auswendig lernen, in dem das Wort vorkommt,
- dir eine Eselsbrücke ausdenken, z. B. einen Reim,
- an ein Ereignis denken, das mit dem Wort zusammenhängt, ...

Opposites

7 textbook p. 85, 9

Find the opposite pairs in the two boxes. Write down the pairs.
Finde die Gegensatzpaare in den zwei Kästen. Schreibe die Paare auf.

customer · healthy · spend · will · different · special

similar · shop assistant · regular · earn · ill · won't

What do we need?

8 textbook p. 85, 9

***air*, *er* or *ar*? Fill in the missing letters.** *air*, *er* oder *ar*? Trage die fehlenden Buchstaben ein.

r e p _ _ _ h _ _ _ d r e s s _ _

m _ _ r i e d s i m i l _ _

s i n g _ _ c u s t o m _ _

New words and phrases

9 textbook p. 87, 14

Fill in the missing words. Trage die fehlenden Wörter ein.

1 Ein **Tierarzt** / Eine **Tierärztin** untersucht Tiere und Haustiere, wenn sie krank sind.

A ____________________ checks animals and pets when they are ill.

2 Ein **Entwurf** ist eine Idee oder ein Plan. A ____________________ is an idea or a plan.

3 Ein **Krankenhaus** ist ein Ort, an dem Krankenpfleger und Krankenschwestern arbeiten.

A ____________________ is a place where nurses work.

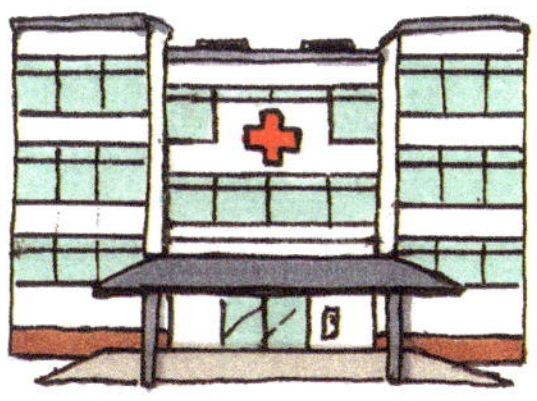

4 Eine **Erfindung** ist etwas Neues, das vorher noch nicht da war.

An ____________________ is something new that did not exist before.

5 **Reisen** ist das, was Menschen tun, wenn sie irgendwohin fahren, um andere Orte zu sehen.

____________________ is what people do when they go somewhere to see other places.

6 Eine **Strophe** ist ein Teil eines Gedichts. A ____________________ is a part of a song.

Adjectives

10a textbook p. 87, 14

Match the adjectives from the box to their phonetic symbols and write them down. What are they in German?
Ordne die Adjektive aus dem Kasten ihrer phonetischen Lautschrift zu und schreibe sie auf. Was bedeuten sie auf Deutsch?

wonderful · smart · ill · similar · honest · regular

1 /smɑːt/ ____________________

2 /ˈregjʊlə/ ____________________

3 /ˈɒnɪst/ ____________________

4 /ˈsɪmɪlə/ ____________________

5 /ˈwʌndəfl/ ____________________

6 /ɪl/ ____________________

10b

Sort the adjectives alphabetically. Add more adjectives from Unit 3. Sortiere die Adjektive alphabetisch. Füge weitere Adjektive aus Kapitel 3 hinzu.

Beim alphabetischen Sortieren guckst du zuerst auf den ersten Buchstaben, bei Wörtern mit dem gleichen Anfangsbuchstaben auf den jeweils zweiten oder sogar dritten. So findest du dich auch in einem Wörterbuch schneller zurecht.

11 textbook p. 89, 18

Solve the crossword. Löse das Kreuzworträtsel.

1 In a city, you have to ... when you need food.

2 You have to ... fires as a firefighter.

3 ... is not as heavy as glass.

4 An actress or actor's job is to ...

5 Many people love ... in their holidays.

6 When you have a job and get money for it, you ... money.

7 A bird can ...

8 If something is nearly the same, it is ...

9 You can put words or numbers into a ... – it's like a list.

10 When you can do something, you are ... to do it.

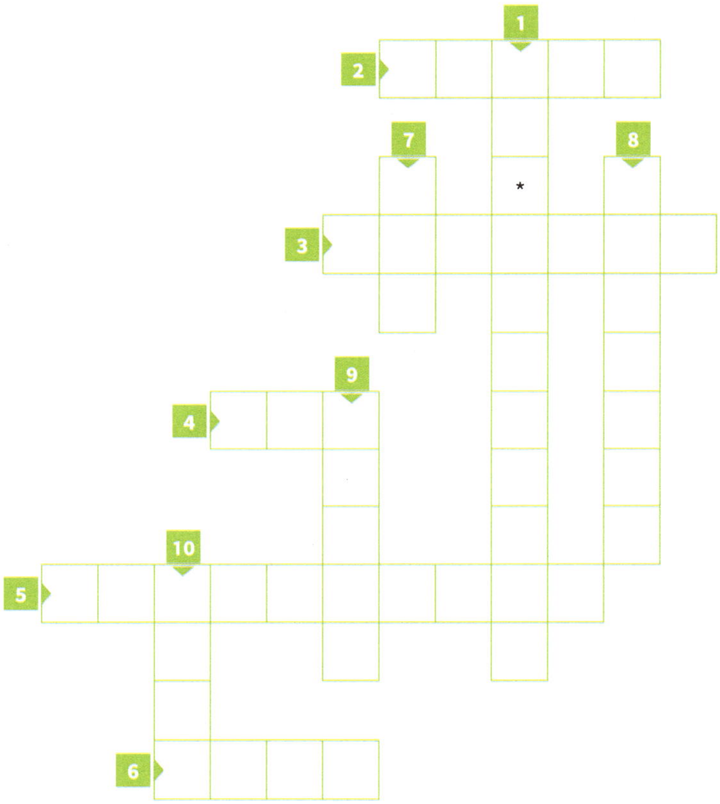

A word snake

12 textbook p. 89, 18

Find the phrases and write them down. Finde die Ausdrücke und schreibe sie auf.

Words and pictures

1 textbook p. 90, 1

Write the right words under the pictures. Schreibe die richtigen Wörter unter die Bilder.

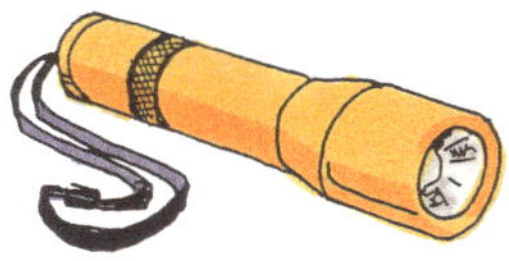

Adjectives and adverbs

2a textbook p. 91, 1

Sort the adjectives alphabetically.
Sortiere die Adjektive alphabetisch.

proud · clear · careful · happy · slow · bright

2b

Now find the adverbs for the adjectives in a).
Finde nun die Adverbien zu den Adjektiven aus a).

2c

Use some of the adverbs from b) to complete the sentences.
Benutze einige Adverbien aus b), um die Sätze zu vervollständigen.

1 She was very proud of her baby brother. She ______ showed his picture to the class.

2 The sun is shining ______ today.

3 She ______ walked home, she was too tired to be fast.

4 A careful person moves very ______ .

Words with missing letters

3 textbook p. 93, 4

C, x or s? Fill in the missing letters. *C, x* oder *s*? Trage die fehlenden Buchstaben ein.

e _ _ i t e d

_ l o w

_ u r p r i _ e d

e _ _ e p t

_ i _ k

_ i n g l e

n e _ t

i n t e r e _ t e d

A word snake

4 textbook p. 94, 5

Find the verbs in the word snake and write them down. Add the German meaning.
Finde die Verben in der Wortschlange und schreibe sie auf. Füge die deutsche Bedeutung hinzu.

Scrambled words

5 textbook p. 94, 5

Unscramble the words and complete the sentences with them.
Ordne die Wörter und vervollständige die Sätze mit ihnen.

1 The opposite of dry is ______ (t – e – w).

2 ______ (k – w – e – a) up! You have to go to school!

3 You have to switch on the light if it is too ______ (k – r – d – a).

4 A good writer can write ______ (l – l – w – e).

5 Are you angry? No, I'm ______ (m – s – y – p – i – l) tired.

6 I don't want to go to the cinema. I would ______ (a – r – h – e – t – r) watch a film at home.

New words and phrases

6 textbook p. 94, 5

Fill in the missing words. Trage die fehlenden Wörter ein.

1 Zuerst wollte ich in den Zoo gehen, dann in den Park, aber **am Ende** bin ich zu Hause geblieben. First I wanted to go to the zoo, then to the park, but ________ I stayed at home.

2 **Früher** lebte ich in England. Jetzt lebe ich in Wales. I ________ live in England. Now I live in Wales.

3 Man hat eine tolle Aussicht vom Turm über die Stadt an einem **klaren** Tag.
You have a great view over the city from the tower on a ________ day.

4 Bienen und Elefanten sind **völlig** unterschiedliche Tiere. Bees and elephants are ________ different animals.

5 **Papier** und **Taschenlampen** sind **Gegenstände**.
________ and ________ are ________.

6 Wenn du jeden Tag zwei Äpfel isst, isst du zwei Äpfel **pro** Tag.
If you eat two apples every day, you eat two apples ________ day.

7 Ich **stehe** jeden Tag sehr früh **auf**. Every day I always ________ very early.

Words and pictures

7 textbook p. 98, 13

Complete the sentences. Vervollständige die Sätze.

You can take photos with a ________.

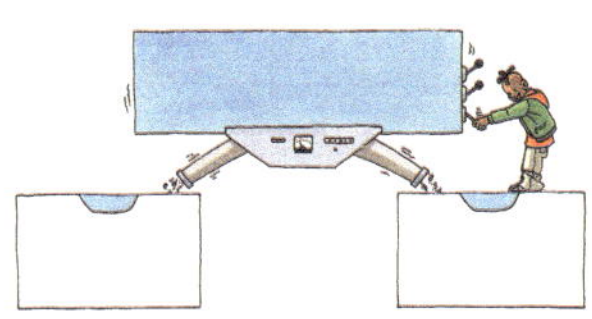

A ________ helps you with your work.

A fire can make loud ________.

Vowels

8a textbook p. 98, 13

Add the vowels *a* or *e* to the following words. Füge die Vokale *a* oder *e* den folgenden Wörtern hinzu.

g _ t

s o _ t h _ t

t r _ n s p o r t

_ x p _ c t

p _ r _ g r _ p h

h _ _ d i n g

p _ p _ r

c l _ _ r

8b

Complete the sentences with the words from a).
Vervollständige die Sätze mit den Wörtern aus a).

Wohlfühlort
Für die Hausaufgaben wie fürs Vokabellernen gilt: Du solltest dich an dem Ort, an dem du arbeitest, wohlfühlen und durch nichts abgelenkt sein!
Eine gewisse Ordnung erleichtert das Arbeiten. Mache regelmäßig Pausen, in denen du zum Beispiel das Fenster öffnest, etwas trinkst und dich bewegst. So kannst du dich besser konzentrieren.

1 I ____________ hungry when I don't eat enough.

2 I didn't ____________ you so soon.

3 Cars or bikes are kinds of ____________ .

4 You can write on a piece of ____________ .

5 A ____________ is a kind of title.

6 The first sentence of a ____________ always starts on a new line.

7 You have a good view from a mountain on a ____________ day.

8 I must do my homework now ____________ I can go to the park later.

Opposites

9 textbook p. 98, 13

Find the opposite pairs in the two boxes. Write down the pairs.
Finde die Gegensatzpaare in den zwei Kästen. Schreibe die Paare auf.

ask · quickly · close · ending · sick · badly

well · healthy · slowly · beginning · reply · open

____

____

____

Words with missing letters

10a textbook p. 99, 14

***I* or *y*? Fill in the missing letters.** *Y* oder *i*? Trage die fehlenden Buchstaben ein.

r e p l _

s _ m p l _

q u _ c k l _

s o m e b o d _

_ m p r o v e

b r _ g h t l _

10b

Write a sentence with each word. Schreibe einen Satz mit jedem Wort.

Classroom phrases

11 textbook p. 99, 14

Match the sentences. Ordne die Sätze einander zu.

1 Take a piece of paper.

2 Read the first paragraph.

3 Match the headings to the paragraphs.

4 Put all the stories together to a book.

5 Write an ending to the story.

6 Collect ideas.

7 Before you start, look at these steps.

8 Present your stories.

A Ordne die Überschriften den Abschnitten zu.

B Stellt alle Geschichten zu einem Buch zusammen.

C Schreibe ein Ende zu der Geschichte.

D Nimm ein Blatt Papier.

E Sammle Ideen.

F Lies den ersten Abschnitt.

G Tragt eure Geschichten vor.

H Sieh dir diese Schritte an, bevor du anfängst.

1	
2	
3	
4	
5	
6	
7	
8	

Vowels

1a textbook p. 104, 2

Add the vowels *a*, *e*, *i*, or *o* to the following words.
Füge die Vokale *a*, *e*, *i*, oder *o* den folgenden Wörtern hinzu.

p l _ y   s t _ p   p _ _ r

_ n c _ _ n t   r _ g h t

h _ m s _ l f   t h _ _ t r _

c _ l l _ c t _ _ n   D _ c t _ r

1b

Complete the sentences with the words from a). Vervollständige die Sätze mit den Wörtern aus a).

1 My brother has a __________ of toy cars. He has many different ones.

2 Turn around. The museum is __________ in front of you.

3 I have a new __________ of socks.

4 The __________ will go on after the break.

5 A lot of people work in a __________, for example actors and actresses.

6 Don't __________ on my foot when we dance together. It really hurts.

7 The book looked __________ and he opened it carefully.

8 He hurt __________ yesterday and had to see __________ Miller.

A word snake

2a textbook p. 106, 5

Find the verbs in the word snake and write them down. Add their German meaning.
Finde die Verben in der Wortschlange und schreibe sie auf. Füge ihre deutsche Bedeutung hinzu.

____

____

2b

Complete the sentences with the words from a). Vervollständige die Sätze mit den Wörtern aus a).

1 You can use my mobile to __________ your friend.

2 Don't __________ on my foot.

3 When you have an idea, you can __________ it.

4 You need to __________ problems.

New words and phrases

3 textbook p. 107, 6

Fill in the missing words. Trage die fehlenden Wörter ein.

1 Du hast den Bus **gerade** verpasst. Tut mir leid. You ______________ missed the bus. Sorry.

2 Wenn man im **Regen** draußen ist, wird man nass.

When you are outside in the ______________, you will get wet.

3 Wenn du **bisher** 50 Bücher gesammelt hast, hast du bis jetzt 50 Bücher gesammelt.

When you have collected 50 books ______________, you have collected 50 books until now.

4 Die Polizeibeamten versuchen den **Fall** zu lösen.

The police officers try to solve the ______________.

5 Die meisten Pferde haben **überall** auf ihrem Körper Haare.

Most horses have hair ______________ their body.

6 Einige Leute tragen im Sommer Hüte oder Kappen auf dem **Kopf.**

Some people wear hats or caps on their ______________ in summer.

7 Die Farbe von **Blut** ist rot. The colour of ______________ is red.

8 Meine Eltern lesen jeden Morgen die **Zeitung**, um herauszufinden, was in der Welt passiert.

My parents read the ______________ every morning to find out what happens in the world.

Words and pictures

4 textbook p. 108, 7

Write the right words under the pictures. Schreibe die richtigen Wörter unter die Bilder.

____

____

____

____

____

Scrambled words

5 textbook p. 110, 11

Unscramble the words and complete the sentences with them.
Ordne die Wörter und vervollständige die Sätze mit ihnen.

1 Read the ______________ (r – e – o – s – c – i – p – t – i – d – n) first before you start playing your new game.

2 Verbs are a ______________ (p – e – y – t) of words.

3 At the airport you often hear ______________ (n – e – n – u – o – t – n – c – m – e – a – n – s) about gates and departures.

4 Getting dressed and eating breakfast are part of ______________ (v – a – d – e – e – r – y – y) life.

5 I have a big ______________ (s – c – r – n – e – e) for my computer now.

6 When you don't give the correct answer, then it's ______________ (g – w – r – n – o).

7 When you ______________ (k – m – a – e) up a story, then it's not a real story.

Odd one out

6a textbook p. 112, 13

Find the odd one out. **Finde das Wort, das nicht zu den anderen passt.**

1 kilogram – hour – minute – second

2 newspaper – design – read – article

3 on – under – in – since

4 play – theatre – open – actor

5 to paint – to put on display – to write – to colour

6b

Complete the sentences with the words from a). **Vervollständige die Sätze mit den Wörtern aus a).**

1 First draw a ______________ for your tree house, then start building it.

2 The museums ______________ lots of pictures on ______________.

3 A famous actress will ______________ the new cinema tomorrow.

4 You need a ______________ of ice-cream and a bottle of milk for the milkshake.

5 I haven't eaten anything ______________ breakfast.

Words with missing letters

7a textbook p. 112, 13

Add the missing double letters to the following words.
Füge die fehlenden Doppelbuchstaben den folgenden Wörtern hinzu.

s c r _ _ n (6, 5)

s u _ _ e s t (4)

a _ _ o u n c e m e n t (3)

c a _ _

c o _ _ e c t i o n (1)

b l _ _ d (2)

7b

What's the new word? Fill in the letters from a).
Wie ist das neue Wort? Trage die Buchstaben aus a) ein.

_ _ _ _ _ _
1 2 3 4 5 6

> Wenn du etwas sagen sollst und dir fällt das richtige Wort nicht ein, versuche mal, es so zu **umschreiben** wie in einem Kreuzworträtsel.

Crossword

8 textbook p. 112, 13

Solve the crossword. Löse das Kreuzworträtsel.

1 the opposite of right
2 very, very old
3 When you collect things, you have a ... of things.
4 When you write down how an object looks, you write a ... of it.
5 a kind of = a ... of
6 1,000 grams is a ...
7 to offer an idea or plan
8 what is between your shoulders
9 When you started something in the past and are still doing it, you have been doing it ...
10 You can watch plays at a ...

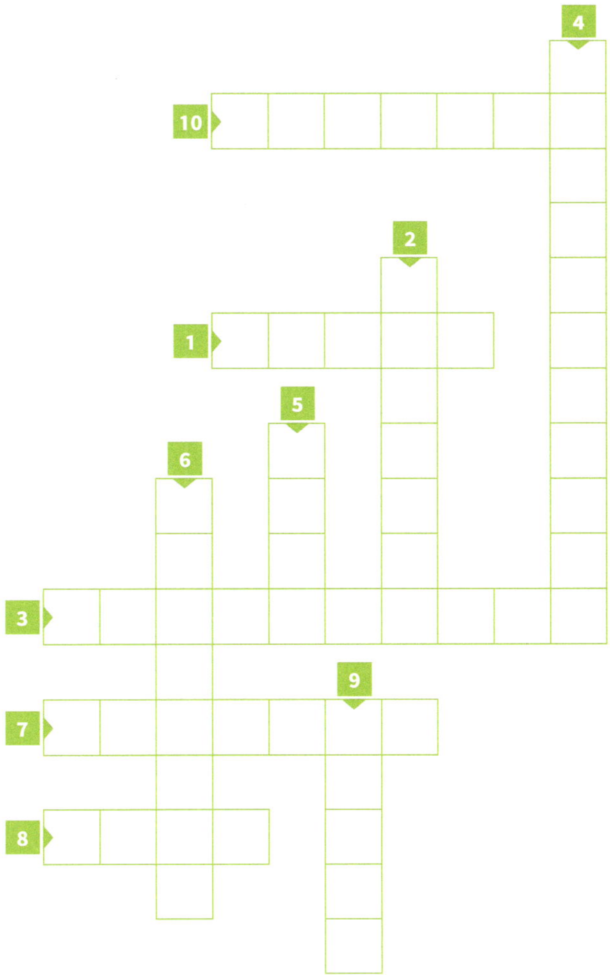

New words and phrases

1 textbook p. 114, 1

Fill in the missing words. Trage die fehlenden Wörter ein.

1 Ein **Programm** ist ein Plan mit Aktivitäten. A ______________ is a plan of activities.

2 Ein **Jugendklub** ist ein Ort, an dem sich junge Leute treffen können und an Aktivitäten teilnehmen können.

A ______________ is a place where young people can meet and take part in activities.

3 In einer **Theater**-AG oder in einem **Kurs** lernt man, wie man ein Theaterstück **aufführt**. At ______________ club or at a ______________ you learn how to ______________ a play.

4 Wenn du wissen willst, was du und deine Freunde machen könnt, kannst du fragen: **Was ist los?** If you want to know what you and your friends can do, you can ask: ______________?

5 Müll muss man **wegwerfen**. You have to ______________ rubbish.

6 Man braucht viel **Übung**, um ein guter Schauspieler / eine gute Schauspielerin zu sein.

You need a lot of ______________ to be a good actor / a good actress.

Combinations

2 textbook p. 116, 6

Achtung! Nicht alle Wörter im rechten Kasten passen.

Find matching pairs. Write them on a piece of paper and add the German meaning. Finde zusammengehörende Paare. Schreibe sie auf ein Blatt Papier und füge die deutsche Bedeutung hinzu.

to take

a photo · notes · place · on display · turns · away · the table · care of · part in · out

The right letter

3a textbook p. 120, 12

C or s? Add the missing letter. C oder s? Füge den fehlenden Buchstaben hinzu.

1 p r a _ t i _ e

2 p e r f o r m a n _ e

3 _ o u r _ e

8 d i _ a p p o i n t e d

4 _ u b j e _ t

7 v o i _ e

5 _ _ r i p t

6 _ o r t

3b

Say the words out loud. What do you notice? Sage die Wörter laut. Was fällt dir auf?

Opposites

4 textbook p. 120, 12

Find the opposite pairs and write them down. Finde die Gegensatzpaare und schreibe sie auf.

happy · to start · everyone · to come back

no one · frustrated · to go away · to stop

Adjectives

5 textbook p. 121, 12

Find the six adjectives in the grid. → ↓ Then choose three of the adjectives and write sentences.
Finde die sechs Adjektive im Gitter. → ↓ Wähle dann drei der Adjektive aus und schreibe Sätze.

L	O	N	E	L	Y	D	R	T	D	A	S	Y	F	D
L	P	Q	D	B	M	V	F	U	L	L	W	S	R	A
R	S	W	W	E	A	X	C	B	T	Z	U	I	U	T
F	P	O	O	J	U	G	P	H	F	D	E	E	S	A
V	D	I	S	A	P	P	O	I	N	T	E	D	T	S
B	W	S	D	A	A	F	O	G	H	B	N	M	R	P
N	Y	C	B	M	Q	E	R	U	U	I	K	L	A	U
I	M	P	O	S	S	I	B	L	E	T	Z	H	T	I
H	A	W	E	R	D	F	T	M	Z	B	V	G	E	G
J	L	U	F	D	A	X	Y	N	W	K	L	G	D	T

Missing vowels

6 textbook p. 121, 12

Add the missing vowels *a, e, i, o* or *u*. Then sort the words alphabetically and add the German meaning.
Füge die fehlenden Vokale *a, e, i, o* oder *u* hinzu. Sortiere dann die Wörter alphabetisch und füge die deutsche Bedeutung hinzu.

1 l _ _ d _ r

2 s _ b j _ c t

3 r _ _ c t

4 s c r _ p t

5 c h _ _ n

6 g _ _ w _ y

7 v _ _ c _

8 s t _ p

9 g _ n _

10 p _ r f _ r m _ n c e

New words and phrases

7 textbook p. 122, 15

Fill in the missing words. Trage die fehlenden Wörter ein.

1 Sie muss immer **weinen**, wenn sie traurige Bücher liest.

She always has to ______________ when she reads sad books.

2 Mein Lehrer sagt "**gut gemacht**", wenn ich eine interessante Präsentation gemacht habe.

My teacher says "______________" when I have done an interesting presentation.

3 Ich konnte meine Jacke nicht finden. Sie war **weg**. I couldn't find my jacket.

It was ______________.

4 Ich trug eine **volle** Tasse Tee zum Tisch.

I carried a ______________ cup of tea to the table.

5 Meine kleine Schwester **spricht** die neuen Wörter sehr lustig **aus**.

My little sister ______________ the new words in a very funny way.

6 Ich war surfen. Was für ein tolles **Gefühl**. I went surfing. What a great ______________.

7 Das T-Shirt **passt** nicht **zu** der Jacke. Ich würde ein anderes auswählen.

The T-Shirt doesn't ______________ the jacket. I would choose another one.

> **!** Es ist viel leichter, sich neue Wörter und Ausdrücke im **Satzzusammenhang** zu merken als einzeln. So weißt du auch gleich, wie sie verwendet werden.

Verbs and nouns

8a textbook p. 122, 15

Match the nouns to the verbs and write down the pairs. Underline the nouns.
Ordne die Hauptwörter den Verben zu und schreibe die Paare auf. Unterstreiche die Hauptwörter.

to sort · to swim · to feel · to answer · to begin · to enter · to end · to perform

performance · feeling · end · beginning · answer · swimming · sort · entrance

8b

Sort the nouns into three groups. Sortiere die Hauptwörter in drei Gruppen.

the same as the verb	ending in -ing	ending in -ance
sort		

Words with double letters

9a textbook p. 122, 16

Add the missing letters *ee*, *ll*, *oo*, *pp*, or *ss*. Füge die fehlenden Buchstaben *ee*, *ll*, *oo*, *pp* oder *ss* hinzu.

1 d i s a _ _ o i n t e d
2 i m p o _ _ i b l e
3 f _ _ l i n g
4 w e _ _ d o n e
5 f u _ _
6 p _ _ r
7 m _ _ d

9b

Choose two of the words and write sentences. Wähle zwei der Wörter aus und schreibe Sätze.

1 ______

2 ______

Classroom phrases

10 textbook p. 123, 17

Match the sentences. Ordne die Sätze einander zu.

1 Make sure you pronounce everything correctly.
2 React to your partner's feedback.
3 Match the German and the English sentences.
4 Look at unit 4.
5 You can work with cue cards.
6 Learn your text by heart.

A Lerne deinen Text auswendig.
B Sieh dir Kapitel 4 an.
C Reagiere auf die Rückmeldung deines Partners / deiner Partnerin.
D Du kannst mit Stichwortkarten arbeiten.
E Achte darauf, dass du alles richtig aussprichst.
F Ordne die deutschen und die englischen Sätze einander zu.

1	
2	
3	
4	
5	
6	

Holidays

DIGITAL+ video 15

textbook p. 160

How can you travel? Write sentences next to the pictures.
Wie kannst du reisen? Schreibe Sätze neben die Bilder.

I can travel by plane.

textbook p. 160

How can the weather be? Write matching adjectives under the pictures. There can be more than one possibility. Wie kann das Wetter sein? Schreibe passende Adjektive unter die Bilder. Es kann mehr als eine Möglichkeit geben.

The weather can be ...

fantastic · great · good · brilliant · perfect · OK · fine · bad · terrible · cold · warm · hot · stormy · rainy · sunny

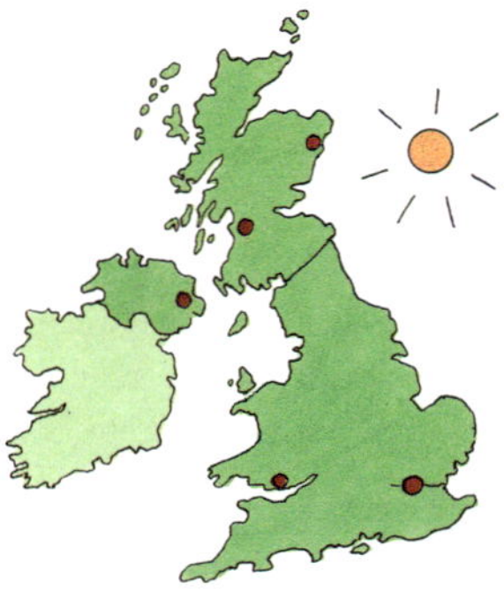

What is the weather like today? Describe it. Wie ist das Wetter heute? Beschreibe es.

textbook p. 160

Write the activity under the pictures. Schreibe die Aktivität unter die Bilder.

1 *go abroad*

2

3

4

5

6

7

8

9

10

11

12

textbook p. 161

Write about what you did in your last holidays.
Schreibe darüber, was du in deinen letzten Ferien gemacht hast.

In my last holidays I went

Getting around

DIGITAL+ video 16

textbook p. 162

Label the London sights. Beschrifte die Londoner Sehenswürdigkeiten.

the Natural History Museum · the River Thames · Hyde Park · Big Ben · the Shard · London Zoo · Buckingham Palace · the London Eye

Complete the sentences with the sights. Vervollständige die Sätze mit den Sehenswürdigkeiten.

1 The King lives in ____________________.

2 The big wheel on one side of the River Thames is called ____________________.

3 ____________________ is a big park in London with over 4000 trees.

4 The River that flows through London is ____________________.

5 A part of the Palace of Westminster is a famous bell called ____________________.

6 You find a lot of wild animals in ____________________.

7 The tallest building in London is ____________________.

8 There is a famous and huge dinosaur exhibition in ____________________.

Giving directions

textbook p. 162

How do you give directions? Label the signs. Wie beschreibst du den Weg? Beschrifte die Schilder.

Celebrations

DIGITAL+ video 17

textbook p. 163

Sort the words into the grid. Sortiere die Wörter in die Tabelle ein.

Easter · Christmas · have a meal · cake · pumpkin · lemonade · orange juice · Christian · Diwali · play games · have fireworks · Easter eggs · sweets · Jewish · Muslim · dress up in costumes · light candles · Chinese New Year · Hanukkah · toffee apple · New Year's Eve · s'mores · meet relatives · jacket potato · have an Easter egg hunt · sing · Bonfire Night · Hindu · biscuits · Eid · chocolate · Ramadan · Hogmanay

festivals and holidays	religion	food and drink	activities

textbook p. 163

Complete the word web. Then write about it. Vervollständige das Wortnetz. Dann schreibe darüber.

My favourite festival is:

traditions

activities

food and drink

My favourite festival is

Rules

textbook p. 164

Write down at least four sentences about what you must or can do or what you mustn't do at these places. Schreibe mindestens vier Sätze darüber auf, was du an diesen Orten machen musst oder kannst oder was du nicht machen darfst.

do your homework · be on time · talk · eat … · run · be quiet · listen to the teacher · use mobile phone · listen to music · be late · wear a school uniform · show respect · …

I must be on time.

I mustn't eat in my room. I must eat in …

Following the rules

textbook p. 164

What are the rules? Write sentences.
Wie lauten die Regeln? Schreibe Sätze.

are not allowed to · mustn't · have to

You are not allowed to feed the horses.

Talking about conflicts

textbook p. 165

Find 14 words for feelings in the grid and sort them alphabetically into the table.
Finde 14 Wörter für Gefühle im Gitter und sortiere sie alphabetisch in die Tabelle.

S	W	A	Q	G	R	I	T	H	T	W	M	E	D	E	D	C
C	R	F	D	C	V	B	N	A	E	M	H	J	L	A	Y	Y
A	N	G	R	Y	H	F	E	P	R	V	E	B	N	N	S	D
R	P	L	K	Q	A	Y	G	P	R	T	X	T	Z	N	U	I
E	L	I	O	O	E	R	F	Y	I	X	C	C	C	O	D	T
D	A	W	O	R	R	I	E	D	B	E	I	A	A	Y	T	I
G	M	N	B	V	C	X	Y	Q	L	W	T	E	R	E	T	R
Z	F	R	U	S	T	R	A	T	E	D	E	S	A	D	X	E
L	K	Z	J	G	B	V	C	A	E	D	D	Q	A	Y	E	D
B	A	D	R	F	V	T	G	B	Z	G	O	O	D	H	N	U
J	M	I	K	O	L	P	N	R	E	L	A	X	E	D	W	Y
E	C	B	O	R	E	D	R	V	T	B	Z	N	U	M	I	L

positive	negative

Write down how you feel. Schreibe auf, wie du dich fühlst.

How do you feel ...

... today?	*Today I feel*
... when you argue with your parents?	*When I argue with my parents I feel*
... when you watch a horror film?	
... when your friends don't have time?	
... when you get a present?	
... when you go on holiday with your family?	

Wildlife

DIGITAL+ video 18

textbook p. 166

Label the pictures. Beschrifte die Bilder.

textbook p. 166

Where can you find which animals? Write sentences.
Wo kann man welche Tiere finden? Schreibe Sätze.

You can find squirrels in a park or in the forest.

What's your favourite animal and where does it live?
Was ist dein Lieblingstier und wo lebt es?

My favourite animal is

Jobs / Talking about the future

DIGITAL+ video 19+20

textbook p. 167

Label the pictures. Beschrifte die Bilder.

What do the people do? Choose six jobs and write sentences.
Was machen die Leute? Wähle sechs Berufe aus und schreibe Sätze.

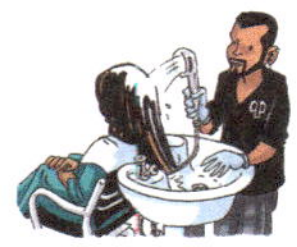

A teacher works at school.

textbook p. 167

What will you do in 20 years? Fill in the word web.
Was wirst du in 20 Jahren machen? Fülle das Wortnetz aus.

family

job

My future

place

Write a short text about your future. Use the word web for help.
Schreibe einen kurzen Text über deine Zukunft. Benutze das Wortnetz als Hilfe.

In twenty years I will

Describing people

textbook p. 168

How can people or animals be? Fill in the adjectives from the box.
Wie können Leute oder Tiere sein? Trage die Adjektive aus dem Kasten ein.

clever · good · friendly · beautiful · fast · bad · nice

1 My brother is a very ____________ runner. He wins nearly every competition.

2 We have a very ____________ parrot. Her name is Ginger and she can speak and sing and she has ____________ feathers.

3 I'm very ____________ at basketball, but I'm really ____________ at swimming. I don't like water.

4 My English teacher is very ____________. We never get homework on Fridays.

5 Our new neighbour is ____________. She always greets us on the street.

textbook p. 168

How can people feel? Match the words to the pictures. There is sometimes more than one possibility.
Wie können sich Menschen fühlen? Ordne die Wörter den Bildern zu. Es gibt manchmal mehr als eine Möglichkeit.

surprised · calm · angry · excited · scared · happy · bored · sick · worried · sad · terrible

____

____

____

____

____

____

____

____

Good style

textbook p. 168

Fill in the words from the box.
Füge die Wörter aus dem Kasten ein.

so that · but (2x) · before · because (2x) · and · or · when

1

2

3

4

5

6

7

8

1 She has to go shopping ______________ she can eat.

2 People can walk around in a park ______________ sit on the grass ______________ talk.

3 They are bored ______________ it is raining and they can't go outside.

4 They always clean the living room ______________ their grandmother comes to visit.

5 He has to go home ______________ it is late.

6 She is hungry ______________ she doesn't like toast.

7 What will happen ______________ she is older?

8 She wants to open the door ______________ she can't.

Write your own sentences with words from the box.
Schreibe deine eigenen Sätze mit Wörtern aus dem Kasten.

Lerntipps

Lerne Verben **zusammen mit möglichen Verbindungen**! Zum einen weißt du dann gleich, wie sie verwendet werden, zum anderen kannst du sie dir leichter merken, weil sie vielleicht auch Bilder im Kopf hervorrufen. Woran denkst du z. B. bei „spend money"?

Schwierige Wörter
Wenn du merkst, dass du bei der Schreibweise einiger englischer Wörter Schwierigkeiten hast, kannst du sie auf ein Blatt Papier schreiben und die Stelle markieren, die dir Probleme macht. Hänge das Blatt in deinem Zimmer auf und gucke dir die Wörter immer wieder an. Du wirst merken, dass du sie bald richtig schreiben kannst.

Gegensätze
Neue Vokabeln kannst du dir auch gut merken, wenn du sie dir mit ihren Gegensätzen zusammenstellst und als Gegensatzpaar lernst. Wie viele Wortpaare kennst du schon?
black – white, right – wrong, pro – con, ...

Für gute Zuhörer
Du kannst dir Vokabeln auch merken, indem du sie dir immer wieder anhörst. Nimm die englischen Wörter auf, die du dir merken willst, und vergiss die deutsche Übersetzung nicht! Höre dir die Wörter regelmäßig an und sprich sie nach.

Verknüpfungen herstellen
Bei Wörtern, die du dir überhaupt nicht merken kannst, kannst du
- ein kleines Bild dazu zeichnen,
- einen Satz auswendig lernen, in dem das Wort vorkommt,
- dir eine Eselsbrücke ausdenken, z. B. einen Reim,
- an ein Ereignis denken, das mit dem Wort zusammenhängt, ...

Wenn du etwas sagen sollst und dir fällt das richtige Wort nicht ein, versuche mal, es so zu **umschreiben** wie in einem Kreuzworträtsel.

Wörterbücher gibt es auch **online** oder als **App**. Du kannst dir oft nicht nur Übersetzungen anzeigen lassen, sondern dir sogar anhören, wie ein Wort ausgesprochen wird. Außerdem findest du hinter dem Wort die phonetische Lautschrift, die dir zeigt, wie das Wort ausgesprochen wird.

Du kannst zum Lernen auch **Wortnetze** zu bestimmten Themen anlegen. Nimm ein Blatt Papier und schreibe das Thema in die Mitte. Welche Wörter passen dazu? Notiere sie und versuche, sie sinnvoll zu verbinden.

Die Strategien, die du zum Lösen von „Odd one out"-Aufgaben nutzt, kannst du auch zum Vokabellernen verwenden: Erstelle in einem Ordner **Tabellen** mit **Oberbegriffen** zu bestimmten Themen. Sammle Wörter, die zum Oberbegriff passen.

Lerne **Verben** möglichst immer zusammen **mit** den **zugehörigen Präpositionen**. Das hilft dir beim Bilden von Sätzen.

Mache sie du deinen Wörtern!
Am besten kannst du dir Wörter merken, die du selbst verwendet hast. Bilde eigene Sätze mit den Wörtern, die du dir merken sollst. Sie können auch lustig sein oder sich reimen.

Wohlfühlort
Für die Hausaufgaben wie fürs Vokabellernen gilt: Du solltest dich an dem Ort, an dem du arbeitest, wohlfühlen und durch nichts abgelenkt sein! Eine gewisse Ordnung erleichtert das Arbeiten. Mache regelmäßig Pausen, in denen du zum Beispiel das Fenster öffnest, etwas trinkst und dich bewegst. So kannst du dich besser konzentrieren.

Es ist viel leichter, sich neue Wörter und Ausdrücke im **Satzzusammenhang** zu merken als einzeln. So weißt du auch gleich, wie sie verwendet werden.